26 STEPS TO SUCCEED IN HOLLYWOOD

... or Any Other Business

26 STEPS TO SUCCEED IN HOLLYWOOD

...or Any Other Business

BEN STEIN AND AL BURTON

HAY HOUSE, INC.
Carlsbad, California
London • Sydney • Johannesburg
Vancouver • Hong Kong • Mumbai

Published and distributed in the United States by: Hay House, Inc.: www.hayhouse.com • **Published and distributed in Australia by:** Hay House Australia Pty. Ltd.: www.hayhouse.com.au • **Published and distributed in the United Kingdom by:** Hay House UK, Ltd.: www.hayhouse.co.uk • **Published and distributed in the Republic of South Africa by:** Hay House SA (Pty), Ltd.: orders@psdprom.co.za • **Distributed in Canada by:** Raincoast: www.raincoast.com • **Published in India by:** Hay House Publications (India) Pvt. Ltd.: www.hayhouseindia.co.in • **Distributed in India by:** Media Star: booksdivision@mediastar.co.in

Editorial supervision: Jill Kramer • *Design:* Tricia Breidenthal

The authors of this book do not dispense medical advice or prescribe the use of any technique as a form of treatment for physical, emotional, or medical problems without the advice of a physician, either directly or indirectly. The intent of the authors is only to offer information of a general nature to help you in your quest for emotional and spiritual well-being. In the event you use any of the information in this book for yourself, which is your constitutional right, the authors and the publisher assume no responsibility for your actions.

Library of Congress Cataloging-in-Publication Data

Stein, Benjamin.
 26 steps to succeed in Hollywood—or any other business / Ben Stein and Al Burton.
 p. cm.
 ISBN-13: 978-1-4019-0700-6 (hardcover)
 ISBN-10: 1-4019-0700-8 (hardcover)
 1. Motion pictures—Vocational guidance. 2. Vocational guidance. I. Title: Twenty-six steps to succeed in Hollywood—or any other business. II. Burton, Al, 1928- III. Title.
 PN1995.9.P75S73 2006
 791.4302'93--dc22   2005025453

ISBN 13: 978-1-4019-0700-6
ISBN 10: 1-4019-0700-8

09 08 07 06   4 3 2 1
1st printing, June 2006

Printed in the United States of America

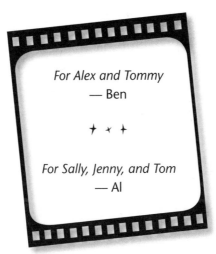

For Alex and Tommy
— Ben

✦ ✦ ✦

For Sally, Jenny, and Tom
— Al

Contents

Foreword

FINDING SUCCESS IN HOLLYWOOD

I am a psychologist by training, and psychologists are more accustomed to looking at Skinner boxes than at Hollywood. A Skinner box, for those who have forgotten their Psych 101, is a box in which rats press a bar in order to receive food pellets (or various other contingencies). I mention this because Hollywood is a gilded Skinner box where some bar presses result in a food pellet coming down the chute (in the form of a life-changing check hitting your bank balance), while still others can deliver an electric shock, and most do absolutely nothing at all. I have had considerable opportunity to observe Ben Stein and Al Burton operating in Hollywood for a number of years now. What I have noticed about them is how many of their bar presses have been of the first variety, the ones that lead to the big payday.

When I met Ben in the mid-1990s, he was better known to me as the author of a sensational self-help book called *Bunkhouse Logic* than as the character actor who immortalized the unlikely line, "Bueller . . . Bueller . . ." In fact, let's stop right here and consider what that already tells us about the path to success through the labyrinth of Hollywood.

"Bueller . . . Bueller . . ." is not exactly a tee up for an Academy Award. It is not "Here's looking at you, kid" or "I coulda been a contender." But Ben took this opportunity and changed it into movie magic, into movie *history.* It was instantly unforgettable, and crashed—if not into Bartlett's—at least into our everyday vocabulary. With two words, every member of the audience suddenly relived all of the high school they thought they had forgotten. It became the single funniest moment of a film studded with hilarious moments. From an actor's point of view, this is not hitting the ball out of the park: This is hitting the jacket off the ball and pulverizing the ball into charmed quarks. Offhand, I cannot think of another example when so much was made out of so little.

Ben Stein did not become a star because of his looks or suntan or charisma. He was given a very tiny opportunity, and he took it to the fourth dimension. This is called adding value to a production, and Hollywood loves people who add value and rewards them copiously. Right there is a major lesson about Hollywood. Do not be a person who stands around the copy machine complaining. Be someone who adds value and you will be loved.

But Ben did not let this overnight success go to his head. He did not thereafter think of himself as the next Olivier and start demanding two star trailers with an attached tanker of Evian water so he could shower in it (as

one star we know did). He did not keep a glove box filled with cocaine and start doing threesomes with the Olsen twins in the back of a limousine in the parking lot at Morton's (or if he did, he never told me about it!). Instead, he maintained an astute sense of his own insignificant place in the Hollywood food chain—an insignificant place that, ultimately, is shared by everyone (for example, Michael Ovitz). I remember proposing some big idea for a show to him once, which he rejected out of hand. Why? "You can't push a string," he told me, matter-of-factly, referring to his own heat quotient at the time. (Incidentally, there is a term in Hollywood for those people who have big ideas for movies and TV shows: They are called *the general public.*)

But Ben made sure he was friendly and easy to deal with, and deal with him people did and people do—again and again. I think that being utterly realistic about his place in the world—neither grandiose nor needlessly self-effacing—has contributed significantly to Ben's mental health over the course of his Hollywood career, which, like all Hollywood careers, is strewn with manic-depressive highs and lows that are practically guaranteed to make you crazy at those times other than when you are being simply ignored, which is most of the time, and which is worse.

I remember going to a meeting once in Al Burton's offices. *Win Ben Stein's Money* was in the development stages, and we were in a conference room running through a prototype of the game in front of a marker board. Ben introduced me to the new guy, Jimmy Kimmel, reading prepared questions off of index cards. When we left that afternoon, Ben told me that he thought one day Jimmy would have Jay Leno's job—a ridiculous-enough prophecy at the time. But this illustrates something else about both Ben's and Al's success: They have x-ray vision for spotting talented people, and they always make sure to associate with them. In Hollywood, success happens by contagious magic. Hang out with losers and guess what? You become one. It is not nice and it is not fair. But it is true.

Another small anecdote: I recall walking down the streets of Beverly Hills with Ben after lunch one day. Ben confided in me that he was worried about money (which is roughly like Scrooge McDuck being worried about money, but never mind.). "I woke up at 3 in the morning with the thought: *What if I never work again?*"

This feeling of dread is ubiquitous in Hollywood, and it is one of the demons that anyone who wants to work in this town must face down again and again. But Ben leads a charmed life, and no sooner had he given voice to this lament than our footsteps were cut off by a car screeching to a halt right in front of us in the alley. Ben's agent jumped out. "Ben, I've been looking everywhere for you. The phone is ringing off the hook! We've got so many deals lined up that I don't know how you're going to fit them all in." You see, there *is* an angel watching over Ben. Maybe it is because he is a Republican. Of course, in Hollywood, it is actually in spite of his being a Republican.

In fact, Ben's worry about having enough money has been extremely productive over the years. It has caused him to work very hard, and it has caused him to prudently save and invest. By way of contrast, all too many people who attain success in Hollywood pour 125 percent of their nouveau riches into current consumption, leading a high-flash lifestyle with results that are almost invariably disastrous. Even if Ben's premonition had been correct, if his phone never rang again, if he never did a single day's work for a day's pay for the rest of his life, it would make no practical difference to his lifestyle whatever. This is the power of saving. It gives Ben what is sometimes called "F.U. money"—although no one should ever under any circumstances leave an employer saying "F.U.," in Hollywood or anywhere. Instead, let's say it gives Ben "No thank-you" money.

There are plenty of producers in Hollywood who are just like the sleazeballs you see parodied on television and in the movies. But by no means are all of them, or even most. Al Burton is soft-spoken, with impeccable manners and an unflinching optimism that he lends to every project. If one idea fails to effervesce, he has 20 more in his briefcase and he goes on to the next (I did mention that these guys are hardworking). And Ben Stein is without doubt the single most generous person I have ever met.

There are astonishingly nice people in Hollywood. If you are a nice person yourself, you are more likely to end up linking up with them. That is just the way it works—not all the time, but enough of the time to make it worth your while.

But wait a minute—I was talking about Ben's classic self-help book *Bunkhouse Logic*—the reason he already was known to me (the psychologist) when I met him. That book catalogued a lifelong interest of Ben's: which attitudes and behaviors generally lead to success in life, and which to failure. In the book before you now, he applies his famous laser-beam intelligence to this same question as it specifically relates to Hollywood.

Hollywood is a small town where everyone knows everyone else, a Disneyland castle protected by a high wall and a wide moat from the barbarian wannabes at the gate. This is the book that lowers the drawbridge. Think of it as a "Maps to the Stars' Homes"—yours.

Do you want to have a successful career in Hollywood? As the Zen master said to his disciple, "The answer is in your hands."

— **Phil DeMuth,**
Hollywood Hills, California

Introduction

Hollywood is a business. To be sure, it is also a fantasy place, la-la land, land of hope and hype, land of sex and sin, world capital of vanity and self-obsession, and land of overused credit cards and underused Bibles. But it is a business, above all. It is a state of mind comprising self-promotion, plastic surgery (the falsely promising silicone breast that looks full of nurture but is in fact a scary mix of toxic chemicals), and yet it is, I must repeat, a business.

It's a business that produces a tanker load of garbage each year and a little bit of art. It keeps the large and the small screen filled with a mixture of genius and discouraging mediocrity. It keeps American youth dancing and swaying and getting high to music filled with violence and danger and self-destruction—and it also produces great, soaring musical experiences (very rarely). But it is . . . a business.

Hollywood exists to make money for the people who work in it. If it happens to make money for its investors, that's great, too. It also happens to create the dominant popular culture in the world, the "Great Satan" that the late Ayatollah Khomeini of Iran used to rail against. The product of Hollywood in terms of music, movies, and TV dominates the ideals and models of young people all around the globe, even in places where the dominant culture is very much aligned against the West. It's an amazing sight to see crowds of angry Iraqi teenagers on the nightly news burning a U.S. truck—while they wear *Rocky* T-shirts. It's stunning to see terrorists wearing Nike hats as they hoist their rocket-propelled grenades.

What Hollywood creates has immense impact all around the world. It's a rare parent in the Western world who has not seen his child consciously modeling her or his behavior on Britney Spears or Brad Pitt, and still, after all these years, trying for the surliness of Marlon Brando or James Dean. What parents have not been frightened and repelled by the language coming out of their kids' stereos as their teenagers blasted rap or hip-hop? And yet, despite its cultural and psychological power, Hollywood is still primarily a business that exists to enrich the people who come here by plane, train, bus, and car, and secondarily, their investors.

We, your humble authors, have toiled in the vineyard of this business for a very long time. Al Burton came to Hollywood as World War II was ending. He has served in positions of authority and creative responsibility for more than 50 years. Among his credits are *Teenage Fair; Mary*

Hartman, Mary Hartman; and the discoveries of Johnny Carson and Scott Baio. He also invented *Win Ben Stein's Money.* He has made a living— and a good one at that—in almost every type of Hollywood endeavor.

Another of his discoveries was your second author, Ben Stein. Al discovered me—I'm writing this Introduction—when we were both participants at a gathering of The Aspen Institute in 1975. Since Al, with the generous contributions of his former boss, the greatest of TV producers, Norman Lear, encouraged me to come to Hollywood, I've been a TV sitcom writer, a movie screenwriter, a film and TV "star," a game-show host, a movie and TV producer, and above all, an observer of the Hollywood scene. Before I came here, I was a reporter, a poverty lawyer, an economist, a trial lawyer, a university professor (talk about a racket), a speechwriter for two Presidents, a columnist and editorial writer for *The Wall Street Journal,* a novelist, and a nonfiction book writer.

Let us assure you, Hollywood is a business. We may have come here with visions of creating great art and living a life outside the bounds of gravity, but we soon learned: *Hollywood is a business.* It's about making money and about getting ahead and making still more money and—this part very rarely happens—having some longevity in the industry.

In this regard, Hollywood is almost identical to the publishing business or the automobile business or the welding business or the insurance business or the garment business or the investment business or even the law or government business. Al and I have seen it up close and personal, and it walks and talks like a business.

Business is about getting ahead by successfully adding value for your employers and also preferably making them look good. That's it—whether you're growing wheat in Archer Falls or writing screenplays.

We (Ben and Al) assume that there are men and women and boys and girls whose goal in life is to get ahead, to make money, and to achieve some measure of job security in Hollywood. We also assume that these are the same goals that sensible people have in other businesses.

After a combined total of about 85 years observing what works and what doesn't in Hollywood, law, publishing, journalism, TV news, and finance, we've come to a few conclusions about how people get successful in business—period. Our experience is mostly in Hollywood and in communications, but we've seen a consistent pattern. The same traits that make for success in Hollywood make for success elsewhere—with some exceptions. (The main one is publicity. It is vital in Hollywood to be talked about. In many other businesses, it is just as valuable *not* to be talked about until you're at a high level of job security and achievement.)

We are in business, too. Our business, at this stage of our lives, is to gather up our observations about life and share them with a larger audience. That's what this book

is about. So without further ado, here are 26 steps we've come up with about how to behave and how to maximize your chance for success . . . and about what works and what does not in Hollywood and any other business.

(And if you're wondering why there are 26 rules and not 25, well, that extra rule might just make all the difference.)

THE 26 STEPS

Develop a Useful Skill

In this world, with very few exceptions, people are employed to produce something. This can be a movie or a TV show or a CD. In order to manifest this sort of production, a prodigious variety of skills and talents are needed. There must be makeup artists, story editors, script writers, prop men and women, sound engineers, video-tape editors, digital-processing editors, and so on. But they all have to have some skill. They cannot just get off the bus and say, "Hey, Hollywood, here I am." They have to be able to add some value by helping to create the finished product, or by working to keep the studios and production companies in business. That can mean doing payroll or health-insurance claims processing—but it has to mean doing something that adds value.

This is especially true with the most visible part of the Hollywood apparatus: actors and actresses. Yes, they have to look good—there's no doubt about that. But they also must have the talent to look like the girl next door or the woman in need of incontinence protection. They have to look like the character the producer or director or ad agency or client is looking for. And they have to show up, know their lines, be well rested, be alert, and be ready for direction.

This type of talent must possess a huge amount of patience and strength of character to put up with the disappointments that are inevitable in Hollywood, as well as the endless frustration of trying to break through to relatively steady employment.

This, again, is true in any business that exists to create and produce a product or service. Unless you can help in that production, you shouldn't even be there. You can, if you wish, go into the one business where just hanging around and being cheery makes for success (such as politics), but that's a greasy pole, to coin a phrase, and when you get to the top, you may not find that there's much fun in sitting on top of a greasy pole.

If you're a pest-control man, you have to know how to find the corners where roaches hang out. If you're a publicist, you have to know where the reporters and columnists hang out. If you're an economist, you have to figure out whether statistics are pointing toward recession or recovery.

Everything—*everything*—is about production of something that people will pay for, either at the counter or through subscriptions or even through taxes. If you can get into your head that you get paid to produce something and that you need a useful skill to do that, you are far, far ahead of the others in the pack.

2

Remember That Education Creates Winners

No one is born knowing how to do the complex tasks involved in adult life. No historian is born with *The Decline and Fall of the Roman Empire* stuck inside his brain. No mathematician, not even the smartest one on Earth, is born knowing the Pythagorean Theorem. In Hollywood, no one is born knowing how Dolby sound works. No one is born knowing how a great screenplay works. No one comes off the bus on Highland Avenue (or wherever the bus stop is these days) knowing how to direct a movie so that the audience is left just hungering for the next scene. Certainly, no one is born knowing how to use an AVID editing system or a payroll-processing machine from IBM.

To learn to do these things, to work these machines or these angles, you have to train yourself. You need instruction from those who have gone before in directing and screenwriting and acting and sound work. This instruction can be at the Yale School of Drama, or it can be under the apprenticeship of someone who's gone before you. Or it can be at a trade or tech school. Whatever it is, you need to have at least *some* training. The training can even be self-directed. I imagine that there are few modes of instruction in screenwriting as potent as reading the scripts of *Gone with the Wind* or *High Noon* or *On Dangerous Ground* (a *film noir* classic that foreshadowed and modeled the whole genre of "bad cop gone good" that led to fantastic wealth and fame for Clint Eastwood, Bruce Willis, and many others).

The point is that you must expect that you'll need training. Don't assume that you were born knowing whatever it is you need to know.

On the other hand—and this is a powerful warning, especially for writers—don't let school bleach out and neutralize your uniqueness. We've seen great natural talent that needed mostly nurturing and encouragement and just the most general outlines of how to succeed whittled down, diluted, and decimated by writing teachers who, to paraphrase a Bob Dylan lyric, would rather get you down in the hole that they're in than raise you up to see your full potential.

Stick to your vision, but allow yourself to be instructed. If the instruction goes against what every instinct tells you is right, go with the instinct.

Again, this is true everywhere. One of our saddest lunches was with a young man who'd inherited a sum of money—about $100,000. That young man went out and bought a computer and a high-speed modem and believed—really believed—that he could start trading stocks and commodities on the Internet. His punishment—and punishment it was, indeed—was to not only lose his inheritance, but also his margin, or what he'd borrowed from the broker, so that his parents had to get a second mortgage on their home to pay off the loan. Had he been given even the most basic instructions on how the stock market works in order to function in a conservative way, that young man could have gone on to make at least a semi-decent return on his money—and he would still have his inheritance.

Life requires instruction—this is fundamental and basic. The director needs instruction—or at least an example of some sort—as much as the accountant. (And by the way, in Hollywood, as writer Joan Didion has pointed out many times, the real art form is what is performed by the lawyers, accountants, and business-affairs people . . . not the writers, directors, and actors. As Ms. Didion so aptly said, in Hollywood, the real art is the art of the deal.) But to do any art at all, some training is vital.

Those who sneer at education are making the biggest mistake that can be made. Natural talent is vital, and so is natural vitality—but training is for those who really believe in themselves and expect to make it.

3

Make Yourself Invaluable

If you're one of the many professionals in town who can make an actor's words intelligible on your sound system, you're in fine shape. But if you're the one who can make the lightsaber sounds of the Jedi knights come out just the way your audience has been yearning for all these 30 years, or close to it, then you're invaluable.

If you're the makeup artist who can make an actress's face look young and dewy under the lights and mask those dark eye bags, you're ahead of the game. But if you can take the 60-year-old pundit and make him look fresh and brand new, then you're far, far ahead of the game. If you're the camera operator who can make the actors see themselves in the monitor and say, "Wow, this is the best I've looked in years," you're going to work constantly.

If you're the development executive who takes home a script and reads it and makes some grunting sounds about it being either good or bad, you'll do okay and may keep your job. If you can give crisp instructions about *why* your reading material from the night before will make either a great movie or a total loss, and offer them with some specificity and incision, you'll soon start moving up the studio totem pole. If your bosses know that you're the one development executive who will definitely get that bag of scripts read and will make comments that are at least as smart as the script—and usually a lot smarter—you can start shopping for that new condo immediately.

You want to be the employee whom the boss asks for and says he must have. This means not just doing a so-so job, but making yourself invaluable. And this brings us to the next step. . . .

4

Know That Good Enough Never Is

In junior high school or high school or even college, it might be good enough to just get by and slide on to the next thing. In some large bureaucracies and in some fast-food places, it might be enough to just be a face in the crowd and be barely good enough not to get fired. There are a lot of mediocre people in this world, and there must be jobs and pastimes for them. Many of them may find work at the California Department of Motor Vehicles, and many others find work at Caltrans. But in Hollywood, or in any other competitive business, there's no such thing as just being barely good enough to get by.

Hollywood is a place that can be likened to a nonstop game of musical chairs. There are simply not enough chairs for all of the people who want to be seated. Or you might compare it to a college where 50 times the number of people apply as can be admitted. (These analogies come to me from my pal Steve Greene, one of the smartest guys I ever met in Hollywood.) In this situation, the least quick, agile, and hardworking are quickly thrown off the merry-go-round, and the most tenacious, quick-witted, and determined stay on. The ones who think they're just going to coast do what all people who are coasting do: They coast downhill. You can't coast uphill, and Hollywood—and all competitive businesses—are all about uphill struggles.

It's a perfectly legitimate life choice to work just hard enough to get by. Enjoying one's leisure time is an under-standable goal. But it's not a life choice that leads to success. If you're just good enough in Hollywood, you'll soon be peacefully unemployed.

This is true everywhere. There may have been a time when just serving time in a large industry, just being there long enough to acquire some seniority, would be enough to move up, even into the world of the executive suite. Maybe that was true in the 1950s, when American industry ruled the world and dominated a Europe and a Far East still busy rising from the ashes of World War II.

But now the world is a savagely competitive place. American industry must be as competitive as the most competitive of our trading partners in Asia and the Far East. That means the men and women who will succeed must mirror that competitiveness in every area of their daily work lives.

Hollywood has always been that competitive. It still is. "Good enough" is a formula for losing a career in the top competitive fields of America. "Good enough" is fine for

a quiet life of anonymity—and this life has its merits to be sure. But for those who want the brass ring in Hollywood or in the armed forces or Wall Street, "the most you can be" trumps "good enough" every day.

5

To Serve Is to Rule

The way men and women get ahead in every field, from the military to Hollywood to politics to the retail industry to agriculture, is to make themselves useful to those above them. When someone starts out in the mail room of a talent agency or a studio or brokerage firm or a department store, this individual cannot bestow favors or privileges or patronage. He or she can only earn merit and advancement by serving those in the upper ranks.

He can make the day of the head of development easier by turning in those great, concise script summaries. She can compile a good list of screenwriting prospects who might be able to write the latest screenplay the studio has in preproduction. He can make sure the agent-boss's star client has a clean, neat limo arranged to take him to the stage. She can write a brilliant story analysis of a book that could be turned into a movie.

To make other people's lives easier is how the beginner gets traction, gets known, and gets valued.

Serving others is how every player at every stage of any career gets ahead. The agent's assistant brings him coffee and makes sure his car is washed and waxed. (And no, in Hollywood you do not take offense if you're asked to do personal tasks for your boss. You do them and you do them as well as you possibly can, and you smile about the opportunity to be of service.)

The agent makes sure that the client's life is easy as he races from city to city doing personal appearances, and listens intently to the client's problems with his son and his love life.

The head of the agency makes sure that her star singing client performs at the senior studio executive's son's bar mitzvah, if only for a few minutes. The CFO makes sure that his studio's most prominent stockholders have the best seats, near the biggest stars, at Hollywood premieres and Oscar parties. The publicist makes sure that his client gets the best seat in the best restaurant in Beverly Hills and sits next to George Clooney. And this is well worth remembering: Ultimately the lighting director, the wardrobe mistress, the agent, the studio executive, the actor, the actress, the producer, the director—all serve the audience. The people who forget this go back to Kankakee pretty soon.

People in the world of Hollywood—and in all other worlds—get ahead by serving others. The senator serves his constituents and donors. The college president serves his star professors and the foundation executives and wealthy alumni that dole out grants to her school. Everyone in the world has to serve someone, as Bob Dylan said. (We love Bob Dylan.)

The chief executive of GE serves the stockholders. The assistant wardrobe designer serves the wardrobe mistress. The parent serves the child. The husband serves the wife. The essence of making yourself meaningful and useful is to serve. The essence of getting ahead is to be extremely useful. The movers and shakers of this universe get to the top of the pyramid by serving. You get nowhere in this world unless you're willing and eager to serve.

Even the President has to serve all of the people. Service to others is what makes men and women indispensable and important in Hollywood and elsewhere. Mao Tse-tung said it, passed on to us by one of our smartest friends, the real estate broker Barron Thomas, and it's true: To serve is to rule.

6

Be Aware That
There's No Quitting Time

Maybe there are clerks at the DMV who can leave work promptly at 5:00. Maybe there are statisticians at the Bureau of Labor Statistics who can come at 8 and leave promptly at 4. Maybe even at a huge employer like Prudential or Lockheed Martin there are clerks who can leave right at quitting time. But in Hollywood, there *is* no quitting time. There's no such thing as saying to your boss that you have to leave because it's the end of the day. You can never say you need to get home to watch the tennis match or the latest installment of *Desperate Housewives.* You cannot even say that you have to get home to your kids. Basically, you can't say, "Hey, I want to have a life."

If you want to make it in Hollywood, you simply have to accept that your job *is* your life. Your career is your life. Your ambition is your life. Your goal in life is to get yourself placed as highly as possible in as short a time as possible. Your goal is not to relax or have "quality time" with your kids or your husband. Your goal is to be as indispensable as possible as fast as possible.

You can read all the articles you want about how the workplace is changing and becoming more people friendly and more family friendly. Maybe it is at the post office, but it's not in Hollywood. You're expected to put the whole rest of your life in a distinctly second position to your career. What your boss wants you to do is what counts, not what your wife wants you to do. Your driven self simply is not allowed to take time off except when you need it for basic and unavoidable recharging of your batteries of your ambition.

You have to work all the time to make it in Hollywood. And you have to work all the time to make it in finance and in the Senate and in the medical world. Your ambition has to be your compelling reason to succeed. If you want to relax, lead a quiet life, and keep up with the local ball club, then you're not cut out for Hollywood. You're not cut out for Wall Street either. You're cut out for being a small-town insurance agent or a bureaucrat, and that's not a dig. Those are perfectly good ways to make a living. There's nothing wrong with them—in fact, I often wish I were one of them. But you have to want success in Hollywood badly enough to give up a great deal of leisure for it. It's a cruel fact, but it's the truth. If you're the kind of gal who wants a balance of work and leisure, you do not want to be in Hollywood. Now you know.

That being said, you're no good to anyone if you're mentally and spiritually exhausted. You need desperately to have your mental and spiritual fountains gurgling and burbling on an ongoing basis. But they won't gurgle and burble if you're exhausted. That's basic. This means that even if you have to pretend that you're going to the library to look up the rights history of a script, even if you have to say that you have too big a stack of scripts to carry to even come in and you have to stay home to read them, you cannot let yourself get exhausted.

And if you're the kind of guy or gal who gets exhausted easily, you should probably not be in Hollywood—or on Wall Street or in Congress. There's not one bit of shame in this. Some individuals have more stamina than others. This doesn't mean that they're better people than others. It just means that they have more stamina. There are plenty of good careers available for those who don't have the roughness and toughness to work around the clock. You belong where you're comfortable, not where you're worn to a frazzle. So work your little heart out in Hollywood, but if it gets you too fatigued too consistently (to the point that you're getting sick a lot), then maybe you should find a different life.

There's a bit of a silver lining here for those who do have the stamina to keep on working day and night. First, if you love your work—as you must love your work to work hard—you will never be bored. Hard work keeps you mentally lively and alert if you have the strength for it. Second, you can go on long and lush vacations when you reach the chairman's office. Then—while keeping a close eye on your back—you'll be able to spend weeks in St. Tropez and Aspen with people who inherited money. But until then, only through the sweat of your brow will you buy your BMW 745.

7

Make Connections— They're *Everything*

There are no Motion Picture College Boards or Scholastic Aptitude Tests to determine who gets into Hollywood and who stays ahead here. Sure, you can go to film school at USC or UCLA and do great things there, and you might get work. But if you're the tennis pro who teaches a major TV and movie producer to win games, you will definitely get a job. (I know this to be true: I've seen it happen more than once.) Even if you're the landscape architect who makes a Hollywood biggie's house in Bel Air look fabulous, you'll almost certainly have a shot at a studio job. If you're the waiter at Morton's who brings the head of the agency his food perfectly done and with perfect timing, you won't be far from a space with your name on it in the studio parking lot.

In Hollywood, as in many chaotic business arenas, connections are everything. I'd like to give you an example of just exactly why this is so. I had the honor of serving as a fund-raiser for a private school my son attended. One of the parents is an executive of a fantastically lucrative firm that does motion-picture insurance. Recently, he needed an assistant. He decided that he'd be a bighearted man of the people and just place an ad in the *Los Angeles Times.* According to him, about 100 young men and women answered the ad. Not one of them could make sensible conversation. Not one of them was even passably polite. Not one of them could form a grammatically correct sentence. Not one of them was dressed decently for the interview. The man said it was inconceivable that any of them could have done the work.

So he just passed out the word among his friends and colleagues that he might be interested in hiring their son or daughter for the job. And what did he find? That every interviewee who came in was nicely dressed, well mannered, and trustworthy. You may say that this is due to their social class, and it probably is. But men and women want people around them who are like them and who are known to them. If this equates to being in the same social class, then so be it. It's all about connections.

There's also something to be said for hiring from within your circle of friends and acquaintances that makes a lot of sense. If you hire a friend's son or daughter, that friend might hire *your* son or daughter when the need arises. Or that person might buy your screenplay or lend you the director she has under contract because you took his son or daughter off the street for the summer. The whole world runs on the principles of back-scratching and log-rolling. People want to do something for those who will do something for them. It won't be any different in Hollywood than it is in Congress or in an investment bank. Why would you even expect it to be?

For example, how did I (this is Ben Stein speaking to you now) get to work in the glamorous and maddening world of screenwriting? I started out as a trial lawyer at the Federal Trade Commission. I was able to move from there to the White House because the people there trusted me even though I had long hippie hair and a mustache.

Why did they trust me? Because my father was President Nixon's Chairman of the Council of Economic Advisers. How did he get that great job? First, he was a super-genius economist. But also, when he was in graduate school at the University of Chicago in the late 1930s, he was pals and schoolmates with the greatest of all economists, Milton Friedman. Friedman later became the main economic guru in Nixon's transition team. It was Friedman who recommended my father, because of that clan connection from the University of Chicago. And through that connection, I got my job at the White House. I was a decent writer, but the connection was everything.

How did I move onward from there? Well, I'd been studying TV as a cultural and political phenomenon for a long time—in fact, since I'd been a student at Yale, and I'd written many essays about it. But how did I break into the bigger world of TV criticism? I wrote an essay and sent it to the op-ed page of *The Wall Street Journal.* I knew I had a shot there because my father had often written for them. Yes, I had a unique angle—that prime-time TV projected major political messages on a consistent basis. No one had been writing about it in that regard since Robert Warshow in *The New Yorker* 20 years earlier. But I got my over-the-transom submission taken seriously because the pooh-bahs there knew my family and might have thought that if my father (a member of their clan) was smart, I might qualify as a member of the clan, too.

I was taken seriously, wrote freelance for *The Wall Street Journal* through my time at the White House, and was then offered a column and an editorship before I was 30 when I left Washington. My beat was mass (or popular) culture, not always from the standpoint of whether it was good or bad, but often in terms of its political and social messages.

When I was covering popular arts for *The Wall Street Journal,* I met and befriended an amazingly smart and likable music executive named Earl McGrath at Atlantic Records. I wrote some favorable pieces about his clients (big, big acts like The Rolling Stones). In turn, he introduced me to my idols, the superwriters Joan Didion and her brilliant and much-missed late husband, John Gregory Dunne. They took a liking to me, perhaps because they were curious to meet someone who had worked for Richard Nixon. Among many, many, many other acts of generosity, they asked their mighty agents, Evarts Ziegler and

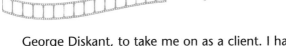

George Diskant, to take me on as a client. I had some of the most well-respected agents in Hollywood representing me from the moment I got off the plane.

As agents, despite their great reputation, they were only pretty good, at least for me. (As an investment advisor, Diskant was superb.) So I needed a new agent. It helped a lot that I already had a famous agency representing me, and that they had already made some sales for me. But again, I needed more aggressive representation. Because I was already inside the clamshell of Hollywood, I soon found myself at a charity lunch for Hollywood players seated next to an man named Michael Ovitz, who was starting a new firm called Creative Artists Agency. Also at the table were my pals Norman Lear and the co-author of this book, Al Burton. They raved about me to Ovitz, he took me on, and soon he was selling my screenplays as fast as I could write them. Maybe faster.

He was the most powerful agent in the history of Hollywood for a time. And Norman Lear was the biggest moneymaker in the history of TV. And Al Burton was the head of production for Lear's mighty company. Their recommendation told Ovitz that I was ready for full clan membership.

How did I become friends with Norman and Al? When I was writing about TV for *The Wall Street Journal,* I wrote two scathing pieces about Norman Lear shows, which prompted Norman to want to meet me. At that time, hardly anyone was heaping anything but praise upon him.

We met and hit it off fantastically well. He invited me to come to Hollywood to write for him then and there, but I wanted to stay at *The Journal.*

A few months later, at a conference on the TV industry at The Aspen Institute, Norman's head of production, Al Burton, showed me a video of a pilot that Norman had made called *Mary Hartman, Mary Hartman.* Even Norman Lear had been unable to sell it despite his TV might. But I loved it and wrote a piece about it in *The Journal* that got it sold in an afternoon. An impartial source had said it was great TV—and it was—and Norman loved me all the more. When I came out to Hollywood, we spent a bit of time together, and Al and I hung out quite a bit, too.

They discovered that I deserved to be an honorary member of their clan because I was respectful to them in person (if not always in print), because I had a sense of humor, and also because I could do things for them. As such, they were ready to help me out with agents, jobs, and their protection.

It all started in 1935 with my father and Milton Friedman at the University of Chicago.

Or, I can put it in an even more interesting way as far as the way Hollywood connections—and all connections—work: When my father worked for Richard Nixon, one of his closest friends was the talented speech writer and *New York Times* columnist Bill Safire. Mr. Safire used to have Seders at his lovely home during Passover, where he'd invite the important Jewish muckety-mucks of

Washington, D.C. My father and mother often took me along, and at one of them, I met a charming man named Eddie Bleier. Ed was a high official of Warner Brothers who had been Bill's roommate at Syracuse University. We talked, and I pitched him an idea for a sequel to *Rebel Without a Cause.* He loved it and bought it for about 50 cents right on the spot, probably because my father was his roommate's pal.

Certainly my being at that august event showed in many different ways that I was a member of his and his roommate's clan. After that, I became friends with Ed's assistant and development chief, a smart young guy named Steve Greene, whom Eddie had assigned the *Rebel* project to. Steve and I spent a lot of time together discussing our Hollywood fantasies. He eventually moved to Hollywood and became pals with a well-known casting executive named Michael Chinich who had become a top executive at Universal Studios. (He's the prototype for one of the characters in *Hurlyburly.)*

Michael and I became pals (and still are). When he was at Universal, he made an offer for my best book ever, *'Ludes,* which is about drug and money addiction. This greatly affected my career because the movie eventually got made (under the title *The Boost*). Then five years later, Michael became head of John Hughes's production company. In that capacity, he introduced me to Hughes. John and I were members of the small but hardy group of Republicans in Hollywood, and we became pals. John and

Michael knew that I'd taught part-time at three universities, so they had me play a teacher in a little gem called *Ferris Bueller's Day Off.* I did a decent job improvising in it, and next thing I knew, I was a star.

Again, it all started with my father and Milton Friedman at the University of Chicago.

To be sure, there were several key points beyond the connections: I had to prove I could do the job—at the White House, at *The Journal,* and in Hollywood. Once I did that, I had to prove I would respect my elders even if I were not on the same page that they were on politically.

They then—again—took me in as a member of their clan.

And this is how connections work.

The problem is when you get off the bus here and have absolutely no connections at all. In those cases, I'm not at all sure where you can start except with a smile and a shoeshine, to coin a phrase.

The newcomer with no connections, waiting tables, detailing cars, doing tour-guide work at Universal Studios has to be the most ingratiating human being on the face of the planet. This brings us to the next rule. . . .

8

There Is No Such Thing as Being Too Likable

Let the losers call this "ass kissing" or "apple polishing." Let them call it any darned thing they want. The fact is that this is how people get won over and influenced to do good things for the apple polisher and the ass kisser.

Nor is this phenomenon a bad, icky thing. We all like people who are kind to us. We all like people who are there with a smile and a pleasant word. We all like listeners, not talkers. We all want shoulders to cry on.

This is how it worked in high school. This is how it worked in your fraternity or sorority. And this is how it works in Hollywood. Plus, this is how it works on Wall Street and in the newsroom and in the halls of Congress.

There's absolutely nothing wrong with being as amiable, patient, and cheerful as is reasonably possible: It gets you where you want to go.

Look at it this way: If George Bush and John Kerry and Ralph Nader have to kiss babies to get ahead, why shouldn't you? If John D. Rockefeller used to give out dimes to cultivate goodwill, why shouldn't you have to smile even when your mouth is tired? If Bill Gates has to set up a foundation and give out billions to be liked, why shouldn't you have to suck up to the people around you? If Tom Cruise feels that he has to act like a chimpanzee on *Oprah* to get publicity for his movie, why shouldn't you have to tell your boss that his hideous paintings are really very fine work?

Who here is old enough to remember Nelson Rockefeller? Here was a man with all of the money in the world, or at least a good chunk of it. When he decided that he wanted to run for President, he had no hesitation about eating chitlins in Harlem, bagels in Brooklyn, and bratwurst in Yorktown. This is how politics works . . . and all of life is politics. We can all learn a wealth of valuable information about getting along and getting ahead from studying politicians at work and on the campaign trail, and if we had to boil down all that information into one phrase, it might well be: *People get ahead by pleasing others.*

It's not a burden either. The amazing thing is that if you do it enough, and if you get into the habit of being ultrafriendly and cheerful to those around you—and especially to those *above* you—you get to like it. When you smile (unless you're in Beverly Hills, where the local religion apparently forbids such expressions), anyone who's sane near you smiles back. When you're cheerful and upbeat around others, they smile at you and are also upbeat and cheerful. This feels good. In fact, it feels darned good.

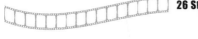

You get into the habit of getting a "fix" of friendliness just by being friendly to those near you. And those people get accustomed to feeling better when *they're* near *you*—and they *want* to be near you.

Rewards, promotion, money—all of these perks are attracted like a bunch of iron filings to friendly, magnetic, cheerful, likable people. Be one and you'll notice that you're soon surrounded by those lovely iron filings.

Only they turn out to be gold.

This is true everywhere. There isn't one job we know of where you get more mileage out of being unfriendly and aloof than out of being cheerful and upbeat. Even in the toughest, meanest dens of trading on Wall Street, you're expected to be congenial with your bosses. Do it and you'll see magic.

9

Get Things Done— and Success Will Flow to You

B oth of your humble authors have seen two types of people (at *least* two types) in Hollywood. The first type comprises those who have huge plans and dreams and schemes. These people are always working on a project that will not just be a movie, but will be the next *Saving Private Ryan*. They're not just working on selling an episodic half hour. No, they want to control the Chinese rights to all of ABC's daytime output. These people are what we might call "wheeler-dealers." They have giant goals and hopes and ambitions. They'll settle for nothing less than the giant score that will catapult them into the league of Harvey Weinstein or Michael Eisner.

We see these people mostly at little coffee shops, at 12-step meetings, and at Denny's restaurants. And they have to borrow money from their friends for lunch.

Money doesn't flow to big dreams and big schemes, and neither does success. At least it flows in that direction

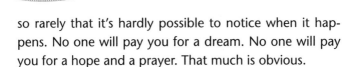

so rarely that it's hardly possible to notice when it happens. No one will pay you for a dream. No one will pay you for a hope and a prayer. That much is obvious.

Then there's the second type of people: those who actually produce something. They write scripts. They write treatments. They do makeup. They carry around scenery and speakers.

More to the point, they have no problem starting out making sure that their boss's caramel macchiato is prepared with exactly the right amount of syrup. And they have no problem picking up their supervisor's dry cleaning or shopping for a birthday present for someone's spouse.

Even more to the point, they take it one little step at a time, and they work their way up in the same fashion: They go from one little job to another little job to a slightly bigger one and on and on.

They have a platform of accomplishment from which to move to the next big thing. They don't presume that they'll just think up something in their spare bedroom that will change the world. They really do know that actually doing something—no matter how small—trumps living on dreams and fantasies.

Look at it in the simplest possible way: Suppose you have a slipping transmission in your car. Whom do you go to when you want it fixed? A man who has a plan he drew up in his basement for a new space-age kind of transmission but has never worked at a transmission shop? Or someone who's done 100 transmission overhauls?

It works the same way in Hollywood (and on Wall Street): Who gets jobs in the studio story-analysis department? The gal who's written thousands of synopses of scripts or the guy who has a scheme for pumping out computer-generated analyses of scripts but has never tested it in real life? You can well guess.

In Hollywood, just like everywhere else, money flows to the men and women who actually produce something, as opposed to those who *pretend* to produce but really just daydream. Overall, success flows to the people who get things done.

Dreamers are fine, and maybe they make good fry cooks at McDonald's. People who think big and disdain day-to-day work are great if their parents can send them money for the rest of their lives. But in Hollywood, on Wall Street, or in Congress, the big red ball of success bounces along underneath the people who actually get things done. Be one of them and you're far ahead of the game—whatever or wherever the game is.

Here again, I'm going to give you a little example out of my own little life. (Ben Stein talking again.) For all of my time here in Hollywood, I've kept myself busy every day doing something. It might be an article that could be made into a movie. Maybe if it were sold, I would get a few thousand dollars. Or it might be a script for an independent producer that also paid only a pittance. Or it might be a voice-over for a cartoon that pays for a car payment. But I always kept busy getting something

"outputted" to the world that showed that I was (a) alive and well, (b) capable of doing something, (c) ready and willing to earn a paycheck, and (d) paying my bills.

All the while I was doing these little tasks, friends had immense schemes and dreams and did *not* work on the little stuff. All of these people, without exception, are now either broke or out of the Hollywood scene or both. The ones who kept their hands in the pie doing small stuff did fantastically well, or at least stayed in the game, which is the same as doing fantastically well, if you can do it all your life.

This brings me, as if by magic, to the next rule. . . .

10

Stay in the Game

I'm going to make this one really short and sweet. Many years ago, my agent read an idea I had for a comedy about two dopey guys getting recruited for the CIA. He sent me over to meet a young producer named Brian Grazer. Brian was a hustling maniac: brilliant, stupendously driven, well connected, and extremely self-assured (except when discussing money). In short order, Brian hooked up my idea with a studio, and we were off to the races.

In Hollywood, there are no straight lines. This meant that the project got thrown off the rails not once but several times. At one such juncture, Brian got the project hooked up with someone else, although at lower rates of pay than we were originally expecting. I complained, and Brian wisely said, "I think the important thing here is to stay in the game."

Later on in this process, Brian threw me off the project, and I had to sue him. But we became friends again, and I, from my lowly perch as freelance writer and commentator, often marvel at this man's amazing success as one of Hollywood's most prodigious and well-paid producers. He's a smart guy (he made *A Beautiful Mind,* among many other fine films), and his smartest comment to me ever was the one about staying in the game.

Hollywood is a small town. I'll say it again. Friends come and go, but enemies accumulate. (Another smart producer named Dimitri Villard told me that one.) It's extremely important to remember that no matter how badly you're wounded, you never want to take your revenge in such a way that you get thrown off the bucking bronco that is Hollywood. You want to stay in the game. Even if you stay in it at a low level. Even if you have to take a cut in pay or prestige . . . stay in the game. That much is vital. Don't write scathing letters. (Suing is fine. It's expected that your partners will steal from you and you'll have to sue. That's part of the game.) Don't write articles saying that everyone in Hollywood is a crook. Just stay in the game. Make your grievances known in a low-key but clear way, but *stay in the game!*

11

Live in Reality

There's a fabulous rock opera from the early 1970s called *Tommy,* by the megagroup the Who (if you don't have it, get it quick on CD). In one of the songs, there's a refrain that basically says: "I'm free, and freedom tastes like reality."

In Hollywood, there's always a temptation to live in a dream world. You can stay at home making up the schemes and plans we mentioned in the previous step and think that you're really making progress. You can have a pitch meeting for a script and some executive can say, "I understand exactly where you're coming from," and you can think this is a sale instead of a brush-off. You can lease a new Mercedes convertible and imagine that you're as rich as Oprah because you have roughly the same kind of car. You can lease a home with a pool and a view overlooking Hollywood and fantasize that you're a star.

These are real temptations and real traps that keep you from living in reality. The reality is that you're doing well if you have money coming in, and lots of it. The reality is that you're doing well if you're having a studio car pick you up early in the morning for your makeup and hair, and then have a studio car take you home at night. The reality is that when Jeffrey Katzenberg calls you to ask that you sell your next script to DreamWorks (the studio he started along with Steven Spielberg and David Geffen) instead of to Paramount, and the head of the latter studio is on the other line making a similar plea, you are successful.

You are not successful if you're spending money to lease the trinkets that make you *look* successful or if you're hanging out at a Jerry's Famous Deli telling people about your meeting schedule. You are successful if you're getting large checks sent to your agent and then forwarded to you, and you're investing them wisely. You are successful if your name appears above the title on a show that's nominated for Emmys and has high ratings.

In general, the number one index of success in Hollywood is money. If you're making it, you're successful. If you're not, you're not successful.

If you're not successful yet—that is, if you're still working your way up the rungs of the Hollywood ladder, don't be dismayed. It can take years—and even decades—to get there. Don't stop trying. But also don't live in a dream world of leased houses and cars that make it seem as if you're successful when you're not. Live in reality. Live with the knowledge that you still have miles to go and many bridges to cross to get to where you need to be. And don't spend yourself into oblivion (more on this later) in a show of make-believe to fool yourself and other people.

Don't pretend that you're above low-level work. Don't pretend that you're a power player when you're still working your way up. And almost *everyone* is still working his way up.

Decades ago, when I (your humble author Ben Stein) was working his way up the Hollywood totem pole, this time as a producer, I had as my partner one of the smartest, most well-liked women in Hollywood. DeAnne Barkley was her name, and she, along with Barry Diller, invented the made-for-TV movie, which used to be a hot item on network TV but has been displaced by HBO and Showtime and TNT movies (which I guess might still be called made-for-TV movies). DeAnne and I traipsed across town from network to network trying to sell our wares. Both of us had lovely Porsches. But as I always reminded her, we weren't important because we had Porsches. The script-buyers were important whether they had Fords or Porsches because they had their checkbooks. To remember that we were basically door-to-door salesmen, despite our fancy cars, put me in just the right frame of mind to sell. We were "beggars in Porsches," as I often said.

On the other hand, Al and I often think of one of the smartest men we've ever known, whom we will call "A." This gentleman wanted to be a screenwriter. He wrote one sex-movie script that got sold, and after that sold nothing. We took him to lunch to see what he was up to, and

he said, "My main decision is that I'm not ever going to be involved in a movie where I don't both write and direct it."

The "beauty" of this comment was that at the time, "A" couldn't even come close to selling a script at all. He didn't even have a spark of the flame of Hollywood heat that's needed for a writer to demand to be the director. He was stone-cold out of the game. Yet he deluded himself that he was a vital player. He made impossible demands. He lived in a dream world. And he never sold a script again, so far as we're aware.

He should have been operating within reality. Instead, he lived and worked and made demands from a cloud of fantasy. This was sad stuff for him and for those of us who love him. Now he's a radio sales agent. He makes a good living, and more power to him. But he locked himself out of the Hollywood game just by living in his fantasy world.

There's a powerful lesson here.

If you're a novice, a "beggar in a Porsche," then behave that way. Don't put on airs. Don't delude yourself. Behave appropriately in relation to your station in the game.

And closely related is . . .

12

Don't Get into Financial Hot Water

It's easy in Hollywood to see the elegant homes of Bel Air, the magnificent beachfront palazzos of Malibu, the gleaming Bentleys on every street in Beverly Hills, and think that you're entitled to live like a rich person. It's easy to read in the fan magazines about celebrities and their expensive purchases and think that you're allowed to buy the same shoes as a $20-million-a-movie star.

There are plenty of people in Hollywood who will sell you that fantasy. They want to lease you the Mercedes convertible. They want to sell you the house with nothing down and an adjustable-rate mortgage. And there are credit-card companies that will sell you anything on the installment plan.

It's easy to spend money in Hollywood, the land of image and the promise of future glories. It's easy to get into debt in a serious way. This is the surest ticket there is to ruination here.

Instead of spending every dime, make sure that you save a big chunk of your wages. The difference between the ones here in Hollywood with the haunted, hunted look—the look of desperation—and the ones who can actually laugh, is that the latter have savings. In the insecure world of Hollywood, you're going to get fired from time to time. Your show will be cancelled. You will be laid off and the boss's niece will replace you. You will find that even the best show you've been working on will be "given a rest," as they said to us when they cancelled *Win Ben Stein's Money*. This means that one day you'll get up in the morning and not have anywhere to go. This means that you won't have a paycheck. But you *will* have rent or a mortgage. You *will* have car payments and insurance premiums.

If you don't have savings, you get genuinely desperate. You begin thinking about taking your clothes off for money or renting your body for cash. We've heard this story not just from one, but from many women, in Hollywood. (We truly don't know what the men do.) You start to think about dealing drugs. (Maybe this *is* what the men do.) You get scared. You get crazy.

Don't let it happen to you. Have savings—as much as you possibly can. No amount of plasma TVs or new cars are worth as much as having savings. It's not square and it's not stupid. It's just basic good sense.

13

Don't Work for an Insanely Abusive Boss

This is Hollywood. Men and women don't come here if they're normal, sensible people. They come here if they're missing some basic part of themselves. They're trying to get it back by applause or money or power. If they were normal, they'd stay home in Cincinnati and work as insurance brokers. If they were normal, they'd be homebuilders in Idaho.

But this is Hollywood, and because the people who come here are *not* normal, they get very angry, very quickly. They think they're Caligula. They think they're Stalin. They want to get absolute obedience and control or else they go crazy. We're not talking about everyone here or even a majority—but we *are* talking about enough of them to make virtually certain that you'll eventually work for one of these madmen (or women).

Don't let them control your life and make you insane. If you have a boss who bullies you or threatens you or

acts nutty, then quit. Do it politely, but by all means do it. There's no reason to put up with abuse on a frightening level. If you take it long enough, you'll start to become insane yourself.

There's every reason to please a decent boss. There's every reason to go beyond the call of duty to get coffee, run errands, and maybe even pick up his spoiled children at preschool. There is perfect sense in staying late to watch dailies with him and then call up Mr Chow to get his dinner reservation, even though you wanted to be home to watch *Jeopardy!* reruns.

And certainly men and women in positions of responsibility are often tightly wound. They're under pressure from their own bosses and from everyone else they do business with. They're human. They can throw fits and act out strangely. That's the human condition. It's the human condition at Paramount and at Joe's Garage Door Repairs. The employee on his or her way up has to deal with it as best he or she can.

But in Hollywood, you can get people who think they're Hitler invading Poland just as easily as you can get a normal man or woman as your boss. You get driven, scared, madly ambitious bosses who have no sympathy for anyone but themselves. To be sure, some of the kindest, sweetest men and women on Earth are also bosses in Hollywood. But there are so many nutcases here in positions of responsibility that you have every likelihood of meeting them and finding yourself working for one or more of them.

No free man or woman deserves to be cursed at unless that man or woman has behaved astonishingly rudely. Let me give you an example: If you're the script reader at a production company and the boss has asked you for notes on a script so that he can have a meeting with the writer, and you've promised to have them on his desk at 9:30 A.M., but you don't even show up at work until 1 o'clock because you were at the Viper Room blowing cocaine and then staying up until five in the morning, and you left your script in the ladies' room at the club, then you deserve to be yelled at.

If, when your boss asked you where the script notes are, you say that you were too high the night before to read the script, you deserve to be yelled at. If your boss tells you he's really unhappy with you and you reply, "Whatever," you deserve to be cursed at. If you openly display contempt for your boss and for your work, you deserve to be berated—you don't belong in Hollywood or anywhere else except a chain gang. But short of that, you should never be screamed at and should quit if you are.

There's a bit of a problem here in this part about abusive bosses. You can't escape them just by seeking your fortune somewhere other than Hollywood. Alas, abusive bosses are found in most high-pressure jobs. If it's a position on Wall Street, in broadcasting, in big business, or at the higher levels of political life, you will almost surely find that you're dealing with extremely high-pressure human beings who are about to explode with suppressed rage and anger.

I (your humble scribe Ben Stein) have seen this over and over again. I've seen it as an observer in Hollywood, where one of the biggest names in TV told two elderly comedy writers that they'd lost their touch and might as well commit suicide—and one of them actually did. The TV superstar didn't even attend the funeral or show the slightest bit of remorse. I've seen it on Wall Street, where I once worked at a moderately prestigious law firm. My supervisor, a man of startling mood changes, once told me that a memo I'd worked on was brilliant. Days later he told me another memo I had submitted to him was "the worst piece of s--t I've ever seen." For the entire summer I was there, I could hear him screaming at underlings.

To this day, I regret that I didn't quit on the spot. I'm sure that my memo was deficient, at least to him, but his manner of expression was unpardonable.

Another colleague of mine, who worked for a major defense-contractor company I shall never identify even if tortured, was told by an irate boss that he would throw her out a skyscraper window because she had questioned a line in one of his speeches. She has been tormented ever since then by the fact that she didn't quit on the spot.

Your dignity is your primary possession—in Hollywood and everywhere else. Don't let it be stolen by a psychopath.

14

Show Loyalty Where It's Due

If someone is good to you, do everything in your power (within the bounds of dignity) to repay that person, and *more* than repay him. Of course, make sure you're there for him (or her) when he needs you. Stick up for him. Do more than the minimum for him.

Loyalty is so rare that, like fine diamonds or emeralds, it is incredibly prized. Stay dignified, of course, but defend that loyalty. It will shine as a mark of rare character in a town where manipulation and treachery are far more the norm.

Not only that, but you'll be paid back for it over the years. The studios and production companies and agencies and networks are staffed at high levels by men and women whose main qualification is their loyalty to someone who rose to a lofty level. Once they've proven themselves trustworthy, their protector will keep them on hand to help him more or less forever. Attach yourself to the people who are good to you, and sooner or later one or more of them will rise to a position where they can make a huge difference in your life—and maybe they're already there.

But again, it's more than just seeking out the main chance. There's also the urgent need for the human soul to seek out those who seem to be loyal—even if they're loyal to someone other than their friends. Loyalty is valued and prized. This is true especially in animals, but even to a greater extent in Hollywood. Loyalty to people who want to be surrounded by faithful friends and helpmates is at least as valuable as talent, and maybe more so.

15

Be Seen

A smart friend said to us just recently that from her position as a casting director, she had two pieces of advice for aspiring actors: (1) Be certain that you have some other reliable source of income; and (2) make sure that you take every moment of the day to be out there and be seen and meet and greet.

Too many would-be actors—and writers and agents—think that they're doing themselves a great big favor by watching several hours of movies every day. They think that if they rent a stack of DVDs and watch them in a darkened apartment, they're making progress.

Maybe they are in some way (progress toward oblivion). But Hollywood, like almost every other business, runs largely via the interaction of human beings. You cannot get a job from a DVD, even from a DVD of the best movie ever made (*Gone with the Wind,* by the way). You cannot get a job from a videotape, even a videotape of the second-best movie ever made (*Blade Runner,* in our estimation).

But you can get a job by painting the home of a power-ful manager. You can get a job by working as a tennis pro at the Brentwood Country Club. You can get a job by waiting tables at Morton's (a very fine restaurant in Beverly Hills).

The idea is to get out there and be seen and have your looks and your intelligence and your helpfulness and your vivacity get noticed.

Herewith, another anecdote, one of many we could use. But this one is especially up-to-date. Years ago, your humble wordsmith, Ben Stein, met a staggeringly beauti-ful girl at the Beverly Center, a big fancy shopping center in L.A. She was amazingly beautiful, just beyond words, and she'd come here from some small town to make her name as an actress. I took her to meet several producers and agents and then lost touch with her. To my delight and amazement, a few days before writing this, I saw her lovely visage on an immense Guess? jeans billboard. Then I looked her up online, and found that she's the cover girl of the August 2005 *Playboy* and also had a role in the hit movie *Wedding Crashers.* And she's also going to be in a forthcoming TV series.

How did she do it? By painting scenery at a studio and being noticed for her amazing face and form. Why didn't it work out when I first met her? Maybe because she was too young or didn't have the acting chops she needed. But she kept going out there and being seen, and eventually, it all worked out to a T.

Her name is Diora Baird, and you will be hearing a lot more about her.

It's tempting in a world as filled with rejection as Hollywood to stay indoors and lick your wounds, or at least be in a spot where you can't get hurt by the many callous and unfeeling people who populate this town and this business. But this temptation has to be resisted. You have to be out "among 'em," as my co-author, Al Burton, likes to say.

This can mean acting for no money in community theaters or working on student films or toiling as a caterer's assistant. It can mean painting scenery. But it has to mean being where people can see you. And meet you. And appreciate you.

The same is true in finance—but in that profession, you have to meet people and they also have to see your work. This means that you shouldn't only have a good personality, but be able to showcase your ideas and insights, preferably in speeches and articles (and even books). You have to get on TV when you can. Your name has to be bandied about as someone who knows useful facts and strategies. Whatever it takes, in Hollywood or finance or politics, *you* are the product. *You* are the service. *You* are what you want to sell or promote to move to the next level. You have to get yourself known to be able to be bought or promoted. That means that no wallflowers need apply.

On the other hand, do whatever you do, but do it with dignity. Yes, some stars have made names for themselves doing porn on boats or in darkened rooms. Yes, some of

them gained notoriety by showing their most personal acts on the Internet. But those are the rare exceptions. Most of the men and women who do porn are deeply unhappy people who never move to a level of anything but increased misery.

Be seen, but be seen with dignity—and *yes,* there is dignity in working at a restaurant or painting backdrops. There is dignity in any kind of legitimate, serious work. Don't ever forget it. There's no dignity at all, however, in shirking work, manipulating those around you, and avoiding responsibility.

16

Don't Use Drugs or Drink Alcohol to Excess, and Don't Smoke

In all of our combined nine decades in Hollywood, we've never seen any behavior that can as clearly and definitively ruin a life as the use of drugs and alcohol. Drugs, even those that some think of as relatively benign, like marijuana, sap willpower, destroy creativity, and make you forget your moral compass. Drugs rob you of your consciousness and your focus. They take you off to a never-never land where you can't concentrate, and where you can't bring your powers to bear on saving your life and delivering your talents to a waiting world.

Drugs make you dependent on them so that your career becomes making the score, not acting or writing or agenting. They drag you down to self-hatred and anger and unfocused rage.

Yes, we can see where they can be tempting. Hollywood is a tough town. There's immense rejection. There's unbelievable tension and uncertainty. Escaping to a place where you don't need to deal with your own consciousness is an immense temptation. Drugs can seem as if they offer an immediate trip to a place where Hollywood can't harm you. But, in fact, they wind up harming you far more than even the cruelest agent or the most officious studio boss.

Drugs aren't glamorous. They're not cool. They're not hip. They're a way of poisoning yourself, shortening your life, ruining your career and your relationships—and breaking your spirit.

The same is true of alcohol that's drunk to excess or if you're allergic to it (in other words, if you're an alcoholic). The temptation is to think that if you drink a lot, you're like Dean Martin and Frank Sinatra. Not true. The temptation is to think that your best friend is alcohol, which is always supposedly there for you no matter what else is happening in your life. The temptation is to think that the natural response to a Friday night after a long and frustrating week is to drink until you black out or wind up in bed with someone whose name you don't recall. Perfectly decent people think that this kind of behavior is rational, even cool.

It's not. Not in the slightest. What *is* cool is to have your wits and your consciousness about you all the time. Not some of the time. Not occasionally. *All* the time. That's what makes for a high-functioning player in Hollywood.

Stay sober if you're the kind of man or woman who can't drink without drinking to excess. Stay sober if you're the kind of man or woman who wakes up the next day and can't remember what you did the night before.

Hollywood (or finance or Congress) is a challenging environment. It takes all you have to make it and to stay made. To fog up your one and only brain with alcohol and drugs isn't the way to make it. You don't write better on booze. You don't make better negotiations on cocaine if you're an agent. You do better sober. It's that clear and that sharp.

That also goes for smoking tobacco. Cigarettes are a powerful drug—we've used them. We know how good a cigarette and a Scotch taste, and how good they make you feel. The power of nicotine is amazing. It can soothe you when you need soothing, pep you up when you need pepping up, and reassure you when you need reassurance.

The problem is that cigarettes cause heart disease, lung cancer, liver cancer, pancreatic cancer, and emphysema. These ailments will kill you sooner or later. They're severe diseases—best avoided if at all possible. Plus, cigarettes make you smell like a transient.

Stay away from demon rum and demon tobacco and demon drugs and you'll come off with heightened mental powers, far better mental and physical health, and much better-smelling clothing and breath.

17

Practice Restraint of Tongue and Pen

You're going to get angry in Hollywood. It's inevitable. Hollywood is not a polite business. Hollywood is filled with rejection—yes, we know we've said it before. Hollywood is filled to the brim with frustration and disappointment.

Very likely, there will be someone who seems like the perfect person to feel angry at: a producer who just gave you notes on your script that you hated, an agent who hasn't returned your calls in weeks, a studio executive who promised he'd have a meeting with you and then cancelled at the very last minute—literally as you were pulling into the parking lot of his building.

Naturally, you feel like dropping the f-bomb all over the place and incinerating half the town with your (very correct and righteous) rage. Of course you feel like calling this person up and screaming at him or sending him an e-mail that's so scorching it will make his computer crash and burn.

Don't do it. If you do, here's what will happen: As sure as shooting, you'll be fired. Then you'll get a new job, and he'll get a new job at the same place—and then you'll need him to approve some other project at his next job. He'll be the one who has life-or-death power over your promotion when he appears in his newest incarnation. Or he'll have lunch with someone who's considering hiring you. Your name will come up. He'll say, "Oh, that jerk called me a motherf----r a few years ago just because I had to go to my aunt's funeral instead of having a meeting with him. I wouldn't touch him with a ten-foot pole."

We've said it before and we'll say it again: This is a small town. If you make friends with everyone you meet, you'll come out smelling like a rose. You won't just be liked, but well liked. If you create enemies—even if your anger is fully justified—you'll have land mines waiting to explode all over town every time you turn around.

People here are sensitive. They don't like being yelled at. They remember it. You may think that they don't care enough to remember, but they do.

If you're disappointed, angry, or frustrated, put it in your memoirs or your diary. Tell your best girlfriend or your father or mother. But don't call up and leave nasty messages or write angry letters.

Friends come and friends go, but enemies accumulate (we know we've said it before, quoting Dimitri Villard, but it's totally true). And in a town as small as this, you don't need any enemies. Decisions are made by people—and

these decisions affect whether you'll succeed or fail. Don't offend these people if it's at all possible.

The same goes for all lucrative businesses and enterprises. There's just no point in needlessly offending people. Politicians who have sharp tongues may get love letters from their avid left- or right-wing fans—but they don't get to be President. Investment bankers famous for burning everyone around them may make their pals laugh, but they don't get to be chairman of Goldman Sachs.

This is basic: Human beings don't like to be yelled at, cursed at, threatened, or even have voices raised at them. Now you know.

Restraint of tongue and pen is golden.

18

Keep Your Eyes on the Prize

Now here's a story that tells volumes in a few paragraphs about how to succeed in Hollywood or anywhere else.

This is your co-author, Ben Stein, signing on again. Long ago, my father entered Williams College, one of the best higher-education institutions in America, as a 15-year-old freshman. He was a stone-solid genius, but very shy. He also had no money to speak of. His father was a skilled tool and die maker at Ford Motor Company, later at General Electric. By the time my pop entered Williams, in magnificent Williamstown, Massachusetts, it was 1931, on the plunge into the Great Depression. His father was unemployed and wouldn't get steady work again for almost nine years. My father had to work at part-time jobs to get through school, even at the rock-bottom tuition rates of those years—plus, he had scholarships. (There were no such things as low-cost federally insured loans or Pell Grants.)

One of the many jobs my father got was as a dish-washer at the Sigma Psi fraternity house. While the well-to-do boys smoked and drank and ate upstairs, my father worked over a steamy hot sink of water, washing dishes in lye-based soap that ate away at his hands. To make the picture complete, Sigma Psi, like all of the frat houses at Williams in those days, didn't admit Jews. So, my father was washing dishes in the basement of a frat house that would not under any circumstances have allowed him to be a member.

When my father recounted this tale to me many years or even decades ago, I said to him, "You must have felt so angry about that."

"I didn't feel angry at all," he answered with his cus-tomary brilliance. "I didn't have the luxury of feeling aggrieved. I was just grateful that I had a job that allowed me to go to a great college in the midst of the Great Depression."

My father got a great education at Williams, then went on to the University of Chicago, and (as I noted pre-viously) went from there to be a famous economist and public-policy expert. He then made it into the cabinet of two Presidents. Later he was on the boards of directors of several public companies. He was able to move from his father's task of working with his hands back to working with his mind. Likewise, he was able to provide a comfort-able (but by no means lavish) life for his family.

This is a parable for life in Hollywood. You will suffer indignities here. You will get asked to do menial tasks far below your abilities. You will be talked to as if you're a dope. You will be talked to by dopes as if you're a dope. You will be talked to by rude people in brusque and unpleasant tones. You will be ripped off. (Sooner or later, everyone in Hollywood is ripped off.) You will go home with your tail between your legs more than once—sometimes more than once a day.

But "keep your eyes on the prize," as the civil rights workers used to sing. Transcend the small stuff, the maddening but petty aggravations that will appear like giant water hazards in your path. Get past the fact that you have a degree in filmmaking and you're being sent to get your boss's car detailed—and she only has her job because she was the mistress of an executive whose wife hated him. Get past the fact that your boss spends several hours each day sobering up after a night with his friends Johnnie Walker and Jim Beam . . . and has breath that would stop a diesel truck cold.

Think of the future. Think of the credentials you're getting. Think of the map you have in your head and how you're moving along that map to the executive suite and to the membership at the Bel-Air Country Club. Unless the indignities are truly humiliating, press on and go for the prize. And remember as you do that everyone suffers insults and offense. *Everyone.* President Bush does. John Kerry does. Nelson Rockefeller did. Bill Gates does. Al Franken does. Jude Law does. Scarlett Johansson does. Even Oprah Winfrey does. It's true. Celebrities do. Studio

executives do. This is the nature of life. It's not just you. It's everyone.

Go past it, realizing that you will endure, that even if you're feeling bad, hurt feelings won't kill you, and surviving them may even make you stronger.

As the spiritual goes: "Keep your eyes on the prize, hold on."

19

Be Patient

There is such a thing in Hollywood (and everywhere else) as the "Myth of the Overnight Sensation." In that tale, the young man fresh out of the Army sits down at a battered typewriter and writes his heart out about his experiences, and it turns out that the book is *From Here to Eternity*. Or a woman sidles up to the counter of a drugstore (yes, drugstores used to have counters where sodas were served) and is discovered to have a great figure under that sweater and signed to a contract at a studio, and young Julia Turner becomes Lana Turner. Or a young man is washing cars in Malibu and does an especially good job washing a powerful agent's Ferrari, the agent takes the man on, and in a month, the new guy is representing stars getting $25 million a picture.

There's a reason these stories are called myths. It's because they represent something, some principle, that human beings wish were true but is not.

The *truth,* as opposed the *myth,* is that in Hollywood, men and women work their way up slowly and methodically, very much like in the military. Now, to be sure, there are fits and starts, and some people start much more quickly than others.

But no one here gets to be a major power player overnight. Some do it soon, but they still work their way up to it. The overnight thing is a sure way to mess up your mind. It's not going to happen, and if you think it will, you'll just get frustrated and angry when it doesn't. So stow away in your powerful brain the knowledge that patience and ladder climbing are very often a fact of life. So often are they a fact of life that there might be said to be an iron-clad law: *There are no overnight sensations in Hollywood or anywhere else.*

Don't expect it, and then you won't get crazy when it doesn't happen. (And it won't.)

20

Don't Talk Endlessly about Yourself

No one wants to hear about your fights with your boyfriend. No one wants to hear about how you need a new washer and dryer. No one wants to hear about how mean your mother was to you when you were a child. At least not now.

No one wants to hear about your arguments with your roommate. No one wants to hear about how upset your stomach is from that sushi you had the night before. The world isn't dying to hear about your weight. The world doesn't care about your complexion or about your new car.

In fact, no one wants to hear you talk at all unless and until you're important enough and famous enough to do them some good, so they *have* to listen to you. That's a basic rule of life.

Most of all, your bosses and co-workers don't want to hear about these fascinating aspects of your life. What the world—including your bosses and co-workers—want

to hear about is their own lives. You confer no value at all upon them by talking about yourself.

However, you do confer extreme value by *listening*. Think about it. If you like it when other people listen to you, then it follows that other people like it when you listen to them. The fact is that you place a burden on your boss if you talk about your life and your troubles. He really doesn't want to hear about it. But you confer a gift on your boss if you're willing to lend an ear to listen to him.

There is such a thing in the world of Hollywood—as in other worlds—as creating "negative utility" in your work. This means that you cost more than you create. You could do this by pilferage or by spending all day talking on the phone to your friends instead of working. Or you could do it by losing files or by forgetting to pass on phone messages.

Obviously, do not do any of these things. But in particular, do not create negative utility by talking endlessly about yourself. No one wants to hear it. Everyone—especially those above you—wants you to listen. Give them that gift and you'll find that the gift is repaid. It means so much to your boss to have an associate who will listen patiently, and he will feel obliged to you and will want you around him in the executive suite. (Of course, by then, you won't have to listen to him anymore!)

21

Get a Rabbi

No, we don't mean that you should convert to Judaism. And we don't mean that you should adopt a man with long sidelocks and a big furry hat and a long coat.

No, what we mean by a rabbi is a guide, a leader, or more aptly, a mentor. That worthy person should be above you in the Hollywood scheme, higher up on the totem pole, but not in any sense a competitor with you. He (or she) should be kindly disposed toward you. He should look upon you as a son or daughter who merits help.

That rabbi should guide you, give you advice, and introduce you to the right people. This person need not be in your company or agency. He can be a friend from a restaurant or a pal from golf or tennis. But he should be able to help you and tell you what paths to take. He should be able to brace you up when you need to make difficult decisions.

Just for example, among us, your authors, Al Burton was for a long time Ben Stein's rabbi and still offers him invaluable advice and insights. Al offered Ben connections and his backing in project after project.

In return, Ben appreciated and worshiped Al for the genius he was and is. The pupil can make crucial contributions to the rabbi, and must do so. He mostly does so by stroking the ego of the rabbi. This is so important to the human animal that it can barely be overestimated. The human being in Hollywood is buffeted by so many storms and gales of tension and uncertainty that if he can get a younger man or woman into his life who constantly tells him or her how great he is, he'll repay the favor in spades. After all, the rabbi has a lifetime of connections and experience to share. It basically costs him nothing to call an old pal and make a connection for his pupil. It costs him nothing to pontificate and offer advice, and in return he gets someone to tell him what a great man and what a great role model he is.

In my life (Ben Stein speaking again) I've seen and heard and heeded many rabbis. One was the great and powerful DeAnne Barkley, whom I mentioned previously. She guided and steadied my footsteps in the world of TV movies. There was also the mighty Jim Bellows, editor extraordinaire and founder of *Entertainment Tonight,* who helped me get on the boards time after time; the uniquely powerful Michael Ovitz, cofounder of Creative Artists Agency and a man of spectacular vision; and Norman Lear, most powerful of all TV producers ever, and a genuinely kind man. And, of course, Al Burton.

Just to give you an idea of what a great rabbi can do for your career, I offer this vignette: Many years ago, I, humble Ben Stein, was having a contretemps with ABC-TV over a made-for-TV movie for which I had written the treatment, or outline.

I couldn't get ABC to agree to what I thought were perfectly basic rules of decent conduct. Instead, they wanted me to capitulate utterly to their demands.

While this madness was raging, I happened to run into Michael Ovitz at Morton's, my favorite restaurant and a major power spot in Hollywood. I asked him what he would recommend. He told me that he had a simple rule of negotiations: "Take a fair position, one that's reasonable to both sides, and stick to it, and you'll eventually get it."

I followed his advice. Respectfully and with humility, I stuck to my position, and sure enough, I got ABC to agree to it.

This is what a rabbi can do for you. Over and over since then, I've stuck to Ovitz's great admonition, and it always works.

Get a rabbi to get you in the door, to tell you what yo do once you get in that door, and to hold your hand and straighten your back up (because, as Martin Luther King, Jr., said, "A man can't ride you unless your back is bent").

If you're kind and grateful and complimentary, you'll be amazed by how easy it is to find a rabbi. (But don't ask us—we have plenty of pupils already.)

22

Keep in Mind That the Most Important Thing about Getting a Job in Hollywood... Is to *Get* the Job

Your two authors, Ben and Al, used to work for the great and powerful (and kindhearted) Norman Lear. Ben was a lowly consultant and creative supervisor, while Al was head of production. One of the most brilliant and successful writing/producing teams within Norman Lear's company, Tandem Productions, which he ran with Jerry Perenchio and Bud Yorkin, was the powerhouse of Schiller and Weiskopf. Bob Schiller and Bob Weiskopf were longtime superwriters in TV comedy. They had both written for *I Love Lucy* (or maybe it was *The Lucy Show*. . . anyway, it was definitely Lucille Ball). They had both written for *All in the Family* and *The Jeffersons* and many other great Norman Lear shows.

Your humble servant Ben Stein was a consultant to them on a funny but short-lived show called *All's Fair*, starring Richard Crenna (R.I.P.) and Bernadette Peters. The two Bobs were fonts of hilarity and insight. Once, Schiller, still very much alive but (I imagine) in permanent mourning since the death of Weiskopf many years ago, said something powerfully epigrammatic about Hollywood: "The only qualification for any job in Hollywood is to get the job."

Let's be cool here. We don't know if Schiller invented the phrase or if it had been around for a while, but it's a killer. It summarizes all the wisdom of Hollywood in 13 words. There is simply no clear, programmatic way to get anywhere in Hollywood. It's like Al Davis's motto for his ragged-but-often-winning Oakland Raiders: "Just win, baby."

You can get there by connections or by luck or by accident or by seniority. You just have to be like a thief running down a hotel corridor trying every lock until he finds one that's open. You have to keep trying as many combinations as you can think of until you get the job you want. Then, once you have it, you can say that you got it through genius or hard work. But meanwhile, you get it how you can get it. And once you have it, you keep it any way you can.

Now, of course, we mean within the bounds of ethics and decency. We don't for an instant mean that you should try to sleep your way to the top. (As our dear pal, the great Phil DeMuth, says, "In Hollywood, you can sleep your way to the middle but not reliably to the top.") We don't mean that you should steal in any way, whether it be money or credits or anything else. You shouldn't covet your neighbor's wife or anything that is not thine. But you should be flexible.

Indeed, if any word describes the personality that makes it in Hollywood, perhaps that word is *flexible,* and in addition to flexibility, you need to have inner mobility. This means that you can motivate yourself to get moving on any project at any time. You need to think of yourself as a quarterback whose pocket is crumbling around him second by nanosecond. He has to pick out a receiver. He has to see if there's a hole in the defensive line. He has to throw or run entirely depending on the circumstances of the moment. But he has to be ready to *move* right away in an instant. And if he turns out to be wrong and gets sacked, he has to be ready to try a new play immediately.

Unethical behavior, never. Ability to be adaptable, flexible, decisive, and able to change that decision in a flash—that's what gets and keeps jobs. To a large extent, ability is assumed (or maybe lack of ability is assumed), and the question is who gets the plum. If it's going to be you, you have to be agreeable, hardworking, always available, tireless, and above all, flexible.

To what extent this is true in other fields is something that may be debated. After all, in law, you need at least a law degree. In medicine, you need at least a medical degree. In finance, you usually need an MBA or a degree in econ. But after that, flexibility and inner mobility are still the keys. After the bare-bones requirements have been met, activity and inner mobility and flexibility and the ability to improvise are the keys.

We'll end this story on a note of supreme innovation, a tale of one of the most powerful producers in the history of the medium. As a young student at USC, he had a job as a gofer at a major studio. Often, he had little to do. So he simply squatted in a vacant office on the floor of big-time producers and pretended to be one himself. As he saw well-known writers come and go, he invited them in to pitch their stories. Soon, he had several fine story ideas lined up and brought them to people at the studio. The studio bit on a couple of them and lo and behold, he was a producer. Now, he supposedly has $200 million, a big fat Oscar, and the respect of his peers—although he also has strange hair.

23

Don't Waste Time with Phonies

This dovetails nicely with the previous step. The sad fact is that anyone in Hollywood can call himself a producer. He can bring in writers and waste their time with promises of studio deals and big-time Hollywood money, when in fact he spends most of his day hanging out at Starbucks or the racetrack. He has no connections, no power, no track record. But he can call himself a producer and lure you in to waste your time.

The same goes for agents. Yes, there is licensure. But many agents basically cannot get their clients arrested. You can go to their offices day after day and demand meetings and auditions, and you'll get pretty promises—but not much else.

Go with the names that are brand names, well-known names, names that get pictures and TV shows made. Stay away from the make-believe men and women who call themselves players but are one small step from being derelicts.

If you haven't heard of a producer or an agent, if your friends haven't heard of him, if he can't refer you to a few well-known names he's handling—stay the heck away.

Time is most of what you have to sell in Hollywood or anywhere else. Don't waste it and get your heart broken hanging around with losers. They will make *you* a loser, too.

Alas, this is all just as true in finance and politics and law. There are a good number of people who talk a good game and might as well be derelicts. In fact, they *are* derelicts. They can't get you into any doors and can only waste your time. So go with the brand names and you won't be sorry.

24

Look the Part, and Look Good

People are judged by their appearance. If they're writers, they can look like total slobs. In fact, they're supposed to look like slobs. But they're supposed to look like slobs getting out of handsome, well-maintained cars. Nothing in Hollywood spells "lost cause" more than showing up in an ancient, beat-up, trash-stuffed vehicle. It's worth the sacrifice to show up in a car that proclaims success. That's your real appearance, your real outward skin. If you're in Hollywood, you are what you drive.

But for agents, neatness and "buttoned-down-ness" are key. For managers and would-be executives—a great appearance that screams investment banker—is basic.

Most of all, for actors and actresses, you simply have to look great.

25

Stand Out Due to the Sheer Excellence of Your Work and Your Enthusiasm for It

We're going to assume that you have some talent for something. (If you don't know what it is, you're in a very big club, and we recommend that you keep searching yourself until you find it.) You have some gift for story-telling (believe us, it doesn't have to be a great gift), so you'll want to be a writer or a producer. You can see a scene in your head as soon as you read it in a script, so you can imagine yourself as a director. You can sell, sell, sell, so you can see yourself as a wildly successful agent. You can make a tousled bedhead look glamorous and sexy, so you can be in hair and makeup. Or you can organize fund-raising, star finding, director finding, and writer finding, so you can imagine yourself as a successful producer.

Or, you love sound and sound effects, so you can be a soundman. Ditto with lights.

Whatever your talent is, you must work at it, hone it, and make that talent sharper and more productive every day. You have to keep up with the trends. You have to learn what is selling and what is not. You have to see who the kids like and don't like.

You have to do the equivalent of what a doctor does when she keeps up with the latest developments in medicine. You have to do what a lawyer does when he keeps up with the latest appellate case law. You have to make sure that your work is excellent and keep it excellent.

This means staying in film and TV school—not the actual ivy-covered campus, but the school that is Hollywood—constantly making certain that you know what's the latest and greatest and being sure you can do it as well as the next guy or girl. And when you do it and keep up and know that you're capable of fine work, stay focused and stay proud of yourself.

There's an old saying in Hollywood that everyone is afraid all the time. Alas, it's true. Afraid of box office failure. Afraid of unemployment. Afraid of losing fame and popularity among the audience. Afraid of gaining weight. Afraid of looking old. Most of all, afraid of losing their touch. John Gregory Dunne, the late and much-missed novelist, essayist, and screenwriter—and good friend—once told me that he believed Hemingway committed suicide because he thought he'd lost his literary touch. That level of fear is unusual in Hollywood, but fear is nevertheless epidemic.

If you can stand up for yourself and not be afraid, but be confident in your talent, you can defeat the worst kinds of demons. If you're the beacon of confidence that the frightened turn to, you're well ahead of the game, and the town will flock to your side. Do excellent work, and then be proud and confident in it and in yourself.

There's another old and famous saying about Hollywood: "Nobody knows anything." Not about trends, not about what will work, not about who's hot and who's not, even about what a contract actually says and means.

And this chestnut is also true: "People stumble onto success as well as into failure." But if you can be confident in your abilities and stand out due to the quality of your work, you will at least seem to know something, and you will be wanted and even revered. (That is, until it's clear that *you* don't know anything either, and you should have a lot of savings and a good lawyer to settle out your contract by then. In fact, come to think of it, you should have a good lawyer all the time in Hollywood. You'll need one. People in this town often break their words, and lawyers are a necessary tool of the trade.)

Stay in top productive form and you'll soon find that you're feeling good about yourself and that others feel good about you. If you can't do that—that is, if you're too lazy to keep your skills sharp—try another line of work.

Look for the Good ... and Praise It

We don't for a minute want to pretend that we thought up this great slogan. Far from it. It's from a superfamous 12-step program. But wherever it comes from, this slogan makes great sense for rising in Hollywood or anywhere else in our competitive world. Human beings like to be praised. They like to be spoken to in a positive way. They do not like to be sneered at or jeered at or criticized or belittled. This is true whether they've done anything particularly meritorious or not. They want their appearance to be complimented. They want their children to be complimented. They want—above all—for their work to be praised and loved. Maybe we can say even more than that: They want to be praised and loved themselves.

Now, this is only human, and it's very basic. In fact, there's nothing more basic.

There's just one big problem: Most of the people you meet in Hollywood aren't going to be especially likable, praiseworthy, or meritorious. They're just ordinary people, however slathered with far, far more ambition and aggression than the normal man or woman. They're also a lot more greedy than the ordinary person. And they—as far as we can tell—have a certain amount of disingenuousness to them as well. Oh, and did we tell you that they're not especially talented, by and large? And that their kids tend to be not so cute and lovely, either? (They often do have glorious houses, though, and sometimes very nice cars.)

Never mind. Look for the good and praise it. If you want to be an amateur sleuth—and we all do—take out your magnifying glass and look for something not just good but great about the people you meet or work for in Hollywood. Maybe he's got a great dog, and you can lavish praise on the hound. Maybe she's just gotten her hair done and it no longer looks hideous, so praise that hair as much as you can.

Now at this point we may just have to be honest. (As Mr. Richard Nixon, one of our former bosses, said long ago, "Honesty may not be the best policy, but it's worth trying once in a while.") There may be nothing, or almost nothing, worth praising about the man or woman in question. So now, we may be forced into that old standby: insincere flattery. Do it anyway. It isn't really a sin. It's more like a white lie—not exactly false witness. After all, no one's under oath.

We praise the screenwriter's each and every word. We mutter something about the obvious comparison with

Fitzgerald. We talk breathlessly to the actress/diva about how Vivien Leigh would have envied her most recent performance. We tell the agent that his deals would make Michael Ovitz gape in wonder. We tell the producer that Joe Mankiewicz or Stevie Spielberg never had it so good. We tell the director that Ridley Scott could learn about the auteur theory of cinema from him.

Or, if we're in the TV world, we tell our pals that they're funnier than Jimmy Kimmel, better looking than Jennifer Aniston, hipper than John Mankiewicz, the head writer on *House* (a very hip show on FOX, for those who don't know).

Think of it this way: You wake up and go to sleep wanting to be liked. No, wanting to be loved. You want to be like the favorite guy or gal in high school. You want to get to school that morning and have everyone in the hallways say, "Hey, Ben, how the heck are you? I hope you're coming to the game and to the party afterward. It wouldn't be the same if you didn't make the scene. So please show up."

You want to wake up, go to work, and have your colleagues tell you that the work you do is of superlative quality. You want everyone you meet to ask you if you've been working out. You want everyone you greet to wonder how you can look so young.

Guess what?! *So does every other human being on the planet!*

In particular, that's what your colleagues in Hollywood or Wall Street or in your law firm or in the halls of Congress want to hear. When they do hear it, they like the people they hear it from. That means—to reduce this to the most basic axiom—people will like you if you praise them. Insecure, worried, terrified people will really like it.

Be the one dishing out the praise. Be the voice of positive feelings. You will be loved for it.

There's a powerful corollary to this, so important that it almost deserves a separate entry: *Do not gossip.* Do not gossip at all. Do not join in gossip. Do not relish gossip. Do not trade in gossip. Do not lower yourself to be part of gossip.

First of all, you should be fairly certain that it will get back to whomever you're talking about, and he won't like it. Second, it will get back to him as if you were his most deadly enemy. Third, it cheapens and demeans you.

Gossip is fun and it's juicy and it's also a way to cut short a promising career. *Do not gossip.* It's tempting, but then so is cocaine. It's fun, but then so is smoking. All three are bad for you and everyone around you. Just don't do it. Period, end of sentence, end of thought.

Be positive. Through the night, through the frustration, through the backstabbing, through the muck—*stay positive!*

Afterword

Now you know. Well, at least you know what we know. And even so, we cannot promise success. Hollywood—and all competitive businesses—are tricky and difficult. But you can and must play by the rules, and we've tried to give them to you here. Good luck, and one final word of advice, which is a repeat from Brian Grazer: Very few of us are going to get to be rich and famous. Just to stay in the game is good enough, and to stay in the Hollywood saddle until you retire is plenty of success. Just stay in the game. That is success enough.

And remember far better advice than we can possibly have thought of:

The race is not to the swift,
Nor the battle to the strong,
Nor riches to men of wisdom,
Nor yet favor to men of understanding,
But time and chance happen to them all.
— Ecclesiastes 9:11–12

Have fun . . . and see you on the Sunset Strip.

About the Authors

Ben Stein is a lawyer, economist, screenwriter, TV writer, TV producer, movie producer, actor, and TV commentator; as well as being a novelist, essayist, columnist, and a prolific writer about financial issues. His scene as the boring teacher in *Ferris Bueller's Day Off* has been voted one of the 100 most famous scenes in movie history. He was on *The Wonder Years* for three seasons; and was the host of *Win Ben Stein's Money* on Comedy Central, a show that won seven Emmys, including one for Stein as "Best Game Show Host" (along with his co-host, Jimmy Kimmel).

He wrote the book and the first-draft screenplay for *The Boost;* wrote the story outline and co-produced *Murder in Mississippi,* an award-winning TV movie for CBS; wrote the story for the lengthy miniseries *Amerika* on ABC; and was a judge on *Star Search* for two seasons. He also had a talk show, *Turn Ben Stein On,* on Comedy Central for three seasons.

He is currently a commentator for CBS News and FOX-TV News.

✦ ✦ ✦

Al Burton is a veteran producer, executive, and writer in Hollywood, and has been for more than five decades. He was the creator of *Hollywood A Go-Go, The Teenage Fair,* and *The Oscar Levant Show,* and supervised innumerable shows created by Norman Lear, for whom he was the longtime head of production. He co-created *Charles in Charge, The New Adventures of Lassie,* and *Win Ben Stein's Money,* for which he also won an Emmy. This just scratches the surface of his accomplishments. His main current work is as inspiration and mentor for Ben Stein.

Hay House Titles of Related Interest

All of the above are available at your local bookstore,
or may be ordered by contacting Hay House (see next page).

✦ ✦ ✦

We hope you enjoyed this Hay House book.
If you'd like to receive a free catalog featuring additional
Hay House books and products, or if you'd like information
about the Hay Foundation, please contact:

Hay House, Inc.
P.O. Box 5100
Carlsbad, CA 92018-5100

(760) 431-7695 or **(800) 654-5126**
(760) 431-6948 (fax) or **(800) 650-5115 (fax)**
www.hayhouse.com® • **www.hayfoundation.org**

Published and distributed in Australia by: Hay House Australia Pty. Ltd.
18/36 Ralph St. • Alexandria NSW 2015 • *Phone:* 612-9669-4299
Fax: 612-9669-4144 • www.hayhouse.com.au

Published and distributed in the United Kingdom by:
Hay House UK, Ltd. • 292B Kensal Rd., London W10 5BE
Phone: 44-20-8962-1230 • *Fax:* 44-20-8962-1239 • www.hayhouse.co.uk

Published and distributed in the Republic of South Africa by:
Hay House SA (Pty), Ltd., P.O. Box 990, Witkoppen 2068
Phone/Fax: 27-11-706-6612 • orders@psdprom.co.za

Published in India by: Hay House Publications (India) Pvt. Ltd., 3 Hampton
Court, A-Wing, 123 Wodehouse Rd., Colaba, Mumbai 400005 • *Phone:* 91 (22)
22150557 or 22180533 • *Fax:* 91 (22) 22839619 • www.hayhouseindia.co.in

Distributed in India by: Media Star, 7 Vaswani Mansion, 120 Dinshaw
Vachha Rd., Churchgate, Mumbai 400020 • *Phone:* 91 (22) 22815538-39-40
Fax: 91 (22) 22839619 • booksdivision@mediastar.co.in

Distributed in Canada by: Raincoast • 9050 Shaughnessy St.,
Vancouver, B.C. V6P 6E5 • *Phone:* (604) 323-7100 • *Fax:* (604) 323-2600

✦ ✕ ✦

Tune in to **HayHouseRadio.com®** for the best in inspirational talk radio featuring
top Hay House authors! And, sign up via the Hay House USA Website to receive the
Hay House online newsletter and stay informed about what's going on with your
favorite authors. You'll receive bimonthly announcements about: Discounts and
Offers, Special Events, Product Highlights, Free Excerpts, Giveaways, and more!
www.hayhouse.com®